99f.

POEMS OF CHILDHOOD

POEMS OF CHILDHOOD

Illustrated by Joan Berg Victor

 The C. R. Gibson Company, Publishers
Norwalk, Connecticut

*A complete list of acknowledgments will be
found at the end of this book.*

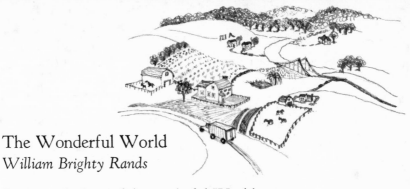

The Wonderful World
William Brighty Rands

Great, wide, beautiful, wonderful World,
With the wonderful water round you curled,
And the wonderful grass upon your breast,
World, you are beautifully dressed.

The wonderful air is over me,
And the wonderful wind is shaking the tree—
It walks on the water, and whirls the mills,
And talks to itself on the top of the hills.

You friendly Earth, how far do you go,
With the wheat fields that nod and the rivers that flow,
With cities and gardens and cliffs and isles,
And the people upon you for thousands of miles?

Ah! you are so great, and I am so small,
I hardly can think of you, World, at all;
And yet, when I said my prayers today,
My mother kissed me, and said, quite gay,

"If the wonderful World is great to you,
And great to Father and Mother, too,
You are more than the Earth, though you are such a dot!
You can love and think, and the Earth cannot!"

House Blessing
Arthur Guiterman

Bless the four corners of this house,
    And be the lintel blest;
And bless the heart and bless the board
    And bless each place of rest;
And bless the door that opens wide
    To stranger as to kin;
And bless each crystal window-pane
    That lets the starlight in;
And bless the rooftree overhead
    And every sturdy wall.
The peace of man, the peace of God,
    The peace of Love on all!

The Magic Window
Eleanor Hammond

Our window is a magic frame
With pictures never twice the same.
Sometimes it frames a sunset sky,
Where clouds of gold and purple lie.
And sometimes, on a windless night,
It holds a great moon round and white.
Sometimes it frames a lawn and flowers,
Where children play through summer hours.
Sometimes, a tree of gold and red
And grass where crisp brown leaves are shed.

And sometimes it shows wind-blown rain
Or snowflakes against the pane.
Our window frames all lovely things
That every changing season brings.

Song for a Little House
Christopher Morley

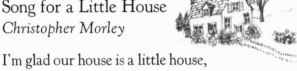

I'm glad our house is a little house,
    Not too tall nor too wide;
I'm glad the hovering butterflies
    Feel free to come inside.

Our little house is a friendly house,
    It is not shy or vain;
It gossips with the talking trees,
    And makes friends with the rain.

And quick leaves cast a shimmer of green
    Against our whited walls,
And in the phlox the courteous bees
    Are paying duty calls.

My Shadow
Robert Louis Stevenson

I have a little shadow that goes in and out with me,
And what can be the use of him is more than I can see.
He is very, very like me from the heels up to the head;
And I see him jump before me, when I jump into my bed.

The funniest thing about him is the way he likes to grow —
Not at all like proper children, which is always very slow;
For he sometimes shoots up taller like an India-rubber ball,
And he sometimes gets so little that there's none of him at all.

He hasn't got a notion of how children ought to play,
And can only make a fool of me in every sort of way.
He stays so close beside me, he's a coward you can see;
I'd think shame to stick to nursie as that shadow sticks to me!

One morning, very early, before the sun was up,
I rose and found the shining dew on every buttercup;
But my lazy little shadow, like an arrant sleepyhead,
Had stayed at home behind me and was fast asleep in bed.

Old Log House
James S. Tippett

On a little green knoll
At the edge of the wood
My great great grandmother's
First house stood.

The house was of logs
My grandmother said
With one big room
And a lean-to shed.

The logs were cut
And the house was raised
By pioneer men
In the olden days.

I like to hear
My grandmother tell
How they built the fireplace
And dug the well.

They split the shingles;
They filled each chink;
It's a house of which
I like to think.

Forever and ever
I wish I could
Live in a house
At the edge of a wood.

Halfway Down

A. A. Milne

Halfway down the stairs
Is a stair
Where I sit.
There isn't any
Other stair
Quite like
It.
I'm not at the bottom,
I'm not at the top;
So this is the stair
Where
I always
Stop.
Halfway up the stairs
Isn't up,
And isn't down.
It isn't in the nursery,
It isn't in the town.
And all sorts of funny thoughts
Run round my head:
"It isn't really
Anywhere!
It's somewhere else
Instead!"

Two in Bed
A. B. Ross

When my brother Tommy
Sleeps in bed with me,
He doubles up
And makes
himself
exactly
like
a
V

And 'cause the bed is not so wide,
A part of him is on my side.

Washing
John Drinkwater

What is all this washing about,
Every day, week in, week out?
From getting up till going to bed,
I'm tired of hearing the same thing said.
Whether I'm dirty or whether I'm not.
Whether the water is cold or hot,
Whether I like or whether I don't,
Whether I will or whether I won't,
"Have you washed your hands, and washed your face?"
I seem to *live* in the washing-place.

Whenever I go for a walk or ride,
As soon as I put my nose inside
The door again, there's some one there
With a sponge and soap, and a lot they care
If I have something better to do,
"Now wash your face and your fingers too."

Before a meal is ever begun,
And after ever a meal is done,
It's time to turn on the waterspout,
Please, what *is* all this washing about?

School-Bell

Eleanor Farjeon

Nine-o'clock Bell!
Nine-o'clock Bell!
All the small children and big ones as well,
Pulling their stockings up, snatching their hats,
Cheeking and grumbling and giving back-chats,
Laughing and quarreling, dropping their things,
These at a snail's pace and those upon wings,
Lagging behind a bit, running ahead,
Waiting at corners for lights to turn red,
    Some of them scurrying,
    Others not worrying,
Carelessly trudging or anxiously hurrying,
All through the streets they are coming pell-mell
    At the Nine o'clock
        Nine-o'clock
        Nine-o'clock
                Bell!

The Land of Counterpane
Robert Louis Stevenson

When I was sick and lay abed,
I had two pillows at my head,
And all my toys beside me lay
To keep me happy all the day.

And sometimes for an hour or so
I watched my leaden soldiers go,
With different uniforms and drills
Among the bedclothes, through the hills;

And sometimes sent my ships in fleets
All up and down among the sheets;
Or brought my trees and houses out
And planted cities all about.

I was the giant great and still
That sits upon the pillow-hill,
And sees before him, dale and plain,
The pleasant Land of Counterpane.

Daddy Fell into the Pond
Alfred Noyes

Everyone grumbled. The sky was grey.
We had nothing to do and nothing to say.
We were nearing the end of a dismal day,
And there seemed to be nothing beyond,
        THEN
    Daddy fell into the pond!

And everyone's face grew merry and bright,
And Timothy danced for sheer delight.
"Give me the camera, quick, oh quick!
He's crawling out of the duckweed." *Click!*

Then the gardener suddenly slapped his knee,
And doubled up, shaking silently,
And the ducks all quacked as if they were daft
And it sounded as if the old drake laughed.

O, there wasn't a thing that didn't respond
        WHEN
    Daddy fell into the pond!

The Land of Story-Books

Robert Louis Stevenson

At evening when the lamp is lit,
Around the fire my parents sit;
They sit at home and talk and sing,
And do not play at anything.

Now, with my little gun I crawl
All in the dark along the wall,
And follow round the forest track
Away behind the sofa back.

There, in the night, where none can spy,
All in my hunter's camp I lie,
And play at books that I have read
Till it is time to go to bed.

These are the hills, these are the woods,
These are my starry solitudes;
And there the river by whose brink
The roaring lions come to drink.

I see the others far away.
As if in firelit camp they lay,
And I, like to an Indian scout,
Around their party prowled about.

So, when my nurse comes in for me,
Home I return across the sea,
And go to bed with backward looks
At my dear land of Story-Books.

Hiding
Dorothy Aldis

I'm hiding, I'm hiding,
    And no one knows where;
For all they can see is my
    Toes and my hair.

And I just heard my father
    Say to my mother —
"But, darling, he must be
    Somewhere or other;

"Have you looked in the inkwell?"
    And Mother said, "Where?"
"In the *inkwell*," said Father. But
    I was not there.

Then "Wait!" cried my Mother —
   "I think that I see
Him under the carpet." But
   It was not me.

"Inside the mirror's
   A pretty good place,"
Said Father and looked, but saw
   Only his face.

"We've hunted," sighed Mother,
   "As hard as we could
And I *am* so afraid that we've
   Lost him for good."

Then I laughed out aloud
   And I wiggled my toes
And Father said — "Look, dear,
   I wonder if those

"Toes could be Benny's?
   There are ten of them, see?"
And they *were* so surprised to find
   Out it was me!

I Meant To Do My Work Today

Richard LeGallienne

I meant to do my work today—
But a brown bird sang in the apple tree,
And a butterfly flitted across the field,
And all the leaves were calling me.

And the wind went sighing over the land
Tossing the grasses to and fro,
And a rainbow held out its shining hand—
So what could I do but laugh and go?

I Want To Know

John Drinkwater

I want to know why when I'm late
For school, they get into a state,
But if invited out to tea
I must'n ever early be.

Why, if I'm eating nice and slow,
It's "Slow-coach, hurry up, you know!"
But if I'm eating nice and quick
It's "Gobble-gobble, you'll be sick!"

Why, when I'm walking in the street
My clothes must always be complete,
While at the seaside I can call
It right with nothing on at all.

Why I must always go to bed
When other people don't instead,
And why I have to say good-night
Always before I'm ready, quite.

Why seeds grow up instead of down,
Why sixpence isn't half a crown,
Why kittens are so quickly cats
And why the angels have no hats.

It seems, however hard they try,
That nobody can tell me why,
So I know really, I suppose,
As much as anybody knows.

The Sugar-Plum Tree
Eugene Field

Have you ever heard of the Sugar-Plum Tree?
    'T is a marvel of great renown!
It blooms on the shore of the Lollipop sea
    In the garden of Shut-Eye Town;
The fruit that it bears is so wondrously sweet
    (As those who have tasted it say)
That good little children have only to eat
    Of that fruit to be happy next day.

When you've got to the tree, you would have a hard time
    To capture the fruit which I sing;
The tree is so tall that no person could climb
    To the boughs where the sugar-plums swing!
But up in that tree sits a chocolate cat,
    And a gingerbread dog prowls below —
And this is the way you contrive to get at
    Those sugar-plums tempting you so:

You say but the word to that gingerbread dog
    And he barks with such terrible zest
That the chocolate cat is at once all agog,
    As her swelling proportions attest.
And the chocolate cat goes cavorting around
    From this leafy limb unto that,
And the sugar-plums tumble, of course, to the ground —
    Hurrah for that chocolate cat!

There are marshmallows, gumdrops, and peppermint canes
    With stripings of scarlet or gold,
And you carry away of the treasure that rains
    As much as your apron can hold!
So come, little child, cuddle closer to me
    In your dainty white nightcap and gown,
And I'll rock you away to that Sugar-Plum Tree
    In the garden of Shut-Eye Town.

Wynken, Blynken, and Nod
Eugene Field

Wynken, Blynken, and Nod one night
   Sailed off in a wooden shoe, —
Sailed on a river of crystal light
   Into a sea of dew.
"Where are you going, and what do you wish?"
   The old moon asked the three.
"We have come to fish for the herring fish
   That live in this beautiful sea;
   Nets of silver and gold have we!"
         Said Wynken,
         Blynken,
         And Nod.

The old moon laughed and sang a song,
   As they rocked in the wooden shoe;
And the wind that sped them all night long
   Ruffled the waves of dew.
The little stars were the herring fish
   That lived in that beautiful sea —
"Now cast your nets wherever you wish, —
   Never afeard are we!"
   So cried the stars to the fishermen three,
         Wynken,
         Blynken,
         And Nod.

All night long their nets they threw
   To the stars in the twinkling foam, —
Then down from the skies came the wooden shoe,
   Bringing the fishermen home:
'Twas all so pretty a sail, it seemed
   As if it could not be;
And some folk thought 'twas a dream they'd dreamed
   Of sailing that beautiful sea;
   But I shall name you the fishermen three:
        Wynken,
        Blynken,
        And Nod.

Wynken and Blynken are two little eyes,
   And Nod is a little head,
And the wooden shoe that sailed the skies
   Is a wee one's trundle-bed;
So shut your eyes while Mother sings
   Of wonderful sights that be,
And you shall see the beautiful things
   As you rock in the misty sea
   Where the old shoe rocked the fishermen three: —
        Wynken,
        Blynken,
        And Nod.

Mr. Nobody
Anonymous

I know a funny little man,
  As quiet as a mouse,
Who does the mischief that is done
  In everybody's house!
There's no one ever sees his face,
  And yet we all agree
That every plate we break was cracked
  By Mr. Nobody.

'Tis he who always tears our books,
  Who leaves the door ajar,
He pulls the buttons from our shirts,
  And scatters pins afar;
That squeaking door will always squeak,
  For prithee, don't you see,
We leave the oiling to be done
  By Mr. Nobody.

The finger marks upon the door
  By none of us are made;
We never leave the blinds unclosed,
  To let the curtains fade.
The ink we never spill; the boots
  That lying round you see
Are not our boots; — they all belong
  To Mr. Nobody.

Boats Sail on the Rivers

Christina Rossetti

Boats sail on the rivers,
    And ships sail on the seas;
But clouds that sail across the sky
    Are prettier far than these.

There are bridges on the rivers,
    As pretty as you please;
But the bow that bridges heaven,
    And overtops the trees,
And builds a road from earth to sky,
    Is prettier far than these.

Thanks

Norman Gale

Thank you very much indeed,
River, for your waving reed;
Hollyhocks, for budding knobs;
Foxgloves, for your velvet fobs;
Pansies, for your silky cheeks;
Chaffinches, for singing beaks;
Spring, for wood anemones
Near the mossy toes of trees;
Summer, for the fruited pear,
Yellowing crab, and cherry fare;
Autumn, for the bearded load,
Hazelnuts along the road;
Winter, for the fairy-tale,
Spitting log and bouncing hail.

But, blest Father, high above,
All these joys are from Thy love;
And Your children everywhere,
Born in palace, lane, or square,
Cry with voices all agreed,
"Thank you very much indeed."

Morning

Emily Dickinson

Will there really be a morning?
   Is there such a thing as day?
Could I see it from the mountains
   If I were as tall as they?

Has it feet like water-lilies?
   Has it feathers like a bird?
Is it brought from famous countries
   Of which I have never heard?

Oh, some scholar! Oh, some sailor!
   Oh, some wise man from the skies!
Please to tell a little pilgrim
   Where the place called morning lies.

The Wind and the Moon

George MacDonald

Said the Wind to the Moon, "I will blow you out;
      You stare
      In the air
    Like a ghost in a chair,
Always looking what I am about;
I hate to be watched; I will blow you out."

The Wind blew hard, and out went the Moon.
      So, deep
      On a heap
    Of clouds to sleep,
Down lay the Wind, and slumbered soon —
Muttering low, "I've done for that Moon."

He turned in his bed; she was there again!
      On high,
      In the sky,
    With her one ghost eye,
The Moon shone white and alive and plain,
Said the Wind, "I will blow you out again."

The Wind blew hard, and the Moon grew dim,
      "With my sledge
      And my wedge
    I have knocked off her edge!
If only I blow right fierce and grim,
The creature will soon be dimmer than dim."

He blew and he blew, and she thinned to a thread.
      "One puff
      More's enough
    To blow her to snuff!
One good puff more where the last was bred,
And glimmer, glimmer, glum will go that thread!"

He blew a great blast and the thread was gone.
      In the air
      Nowhere
    Was a moonbeam bare;
Far-off and harmless the shy stars shone;
Sure and certain the Moon was gone!

The Wind he took to his revels once more;
      On down,
      In town,
    Like a merry-mad clown,
He leaped and hallooed with whistle and roar —
"What's that?" The glimmering thread once more!

He flew in a rage; he danced and blew;
But in vain
Was the pain
Of his bursting brain;
For still the broader the Moon-scrap grew
The broader he swelled his big cheeks and blew.

Slowly she grew, till she filled the night,
And shone
On her throne
In the sky alone,
A matchless, wonderful, silvery light,
Radiant and lovely, the Queen of the night.

Said the Wind, "What a marvel of power am I!"
With my breath,
Good faith,
I blew her to death —
First blew her away right out of the sky —
Then blew her right in; what strength have I!"

But the Moon she knew nothing about the affair;
For high
In the sky,
With her one white eye,
Motionless, miles above the air,
She had never heard the great Wind blare.

The Sun
John Drinkwater

I told the Sun that I was glad,
    I'm sure I don't know why;
Somehow the pleasant way he had
    Of shining in the sky,
Just put a notion in my head
    That wouldn't it be fun
If, walking on the hill, I said
    "I'm happy" to the Sun.

Jack Frost
Helen Bayley Davis

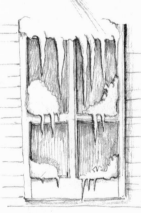

Someone painted pictures on my
    Windowpane last night —
Willow trees with trailing boughs
    And flowers, frosty white,

And lovely crystal butterflies;
    But when the morning sun
Touched them with its golden beams,
    They vanished one by one!

Pippa's Song
Robert Browning

The year's at the spring,
And day's at the morn;
Morning's at seven;
The hillside's dew-pearled;

The lark's on the wing;
The snail's on the thorn:
God's in His Heaven—
All's right with the world!

A Comparison
John Farrar

Apple blossoms look like snow,
They're different, though.
Snow falls softly, but it brings
Noisy things:
Sleighs and bells, forts and fights,
Cosy nights.
But apple blossoms when they go,
White and slow,
Quiet all the orchard space
Till the place
Hushed with falling sweetness seems
Filled with dreams.

Mud

Polly Chase Boyden

Mud is very nice to feel
    All squishy-squash between the toes!
I'd rather wade in wiggly mud
    Than smell a yellow rose.

Nobody else but the rosebush knows
How nice mud feels
    Between the toes.

A Vagabond Song
Bliss Carman

There is something in the autumn that
    is native to my blood —
Touch of manner, hint of mood;
And my heart is like a rhyme,
With the yellow and the purple and
    the crimson keeping time.

The scarlet of the maples can shake me
    like a cry
Of bugles going by.
And my lonely spirit thrills
To see the frosty asters like a smoke
    upon the hills.

There is something in October sets the
    gypsy blood astir;
We must rise and follow her,
When from every hill of flame
She calls and calls each vagabond by
    name.

Autumn Fancies

Unknown

The maple is a dainty maid,
   The pet of all the wood,
Who lights the dusky forest glade
   With scarlet cloak and hood.

The elm a lovely lady is,
   In shimmering robes of gold,
That catch the sunlight when she moves,
   And glisten, fold on fold.

The sumac is a gypsy queen,
   Who flaunts in crimson dressed,
And wild along the roadside runs,
   Red blossoms in her breast.

And towering high above the wood,
   All in his purple cloak,
A monarch in his splendor is
   The proud and princely oak.

May-Day Song

The moon shines bright; the stars give a light
    A little before 'tis day:
So God bless you all, both great and small,
    And send you a joyful May.

We have been rambling all the night,
    And almost all the day;
And now, returning back again,
    We have brought you a branch of May.

A branch of May we have brought you,
   And at your door it stands;
It is but a sprout, but it's well budded out
   By the work of our Lord's hands.

The hedges and trees they are so green,
   As green as any leek;
Our heavenly Father He watered them
   With His heavenly dew so sweet.

The heavenly gates are open wide,
   Our paths are beaten plain;
And if a man be not too far gone,
   He may return again.

The moon shines bright; the stars give a light,
   A little before 'tis day:
So God bless you all, both great and small,
   And send you a joyful May!

Summer Days
Christina Rossetti

Winter is cold-hearted;
   Spring is yea and nay;
Autumn is a weathercock,
   Blown every way:
Summer days for me,
When every leaf is on its tree,

When Robin's not a beggar,
   And Jenny Wren's a bride,
And larks hang, singing, singing,
    singing,
   Over the wheat-fields wide,
   And anchored lilies ride,
And the pendulum spider
   Swings from side to side,

And blue-black beetles transact
    business,
   And gnats fly in a host,
And furry caterpillars hasten
   That no time be lost,
And moths grow fat and thrive,
And ladybirds arrive.

Before green apples blush,
  Before green nuts embrown,
Why, one day in the country
  Is worth a month in town —
  Is worth a day and a year
Of the dusty, musty, lag-last fashion
  That days drone elsewhere.

How the Leaves Came Down
Susan Coolidge

I'll tell you how the leaves came down.
  The great Tree to his children said:
"You're getting sleepy, Yellow and Brown,
  Yes, very sleepy, little Red.
  It is quite time to go to bed."

"Ah!" begged each silly, pouting leaf,
  "Let us a little longer stay;
Dear Father Tree, behold our grief!
  'Tis such a very pleasant day,
  We do not want to go away."

So, just for one more merry day
  To the great Tree the leaflets clung,
Frolicked and danced, and had their way,
  Upon the autumn breezes swung,
  Whispering all their sports among —

"Perhaps the great Tree will forget,
  And let us stay until the spring,
If we all beg, and coax, and fret."
  But the great Tree did no such thing;
  He smiled to hear their whispering.

"Come, children, all to bed," he cried;
  And ere the leaves could urge their prayer,
He shook his head, and far and wide,
  Fluttering and rustling everywhere,
  Down sped the leaflets through the air.

I saw them; on the ground they lay,
  Golden and red, a huddled swarm,
Waiting till one from far away,
  White bedclothes heaped upon her arm,
  Should come to wrap them safe and warm.

The great bare Tree looked down and smiled.
  "Good night, dear little leaves," he said.
And from below each sleepy child
  Replied, "Good night," and murmured,
  "It is *so* nice to go to bed!"

White Fields
James Stephens

1.
In the winter time we go
Walking in the fields of snow;

Where there is no grass at all;
Where the top of every wall,

Every fence and every tree,
Is as white as white can be.

2.
Pointing out the way we came,
Everyone of them the same —

All across the fields there be
Prints in silver filigree;

And our mothers always know,
By our footprints in the snow,

Where the children go.

The Snow
Emily Dickinson

It sifts from leaden sieves,
It powders all the wood,
It fills with alabaster wool
The wrinkles of the road.

It makes an even face
Of mountain and of plain, —
Unbroken forehead from the east
Unto the east again.

It reaches to the fence,
It wraps it, rail by rail,
Till it is lost in fleeces;
It flings a crystal veil

On stump and stack and stem, —
The summer's empty room,
Acres of seams where harvests were,
Recordless, but for them.

It ruffles wrists of posts,
As ankles of a queen, —
Then stills its artisans like ghosts,
Denying they have been.

Skating
Herbert Asquith

When I try to skate,
My feet are so wary
They grit and they grate:
And then I watch Mary
Easily gliding,
Like an ice-fairy;
Skimming and curving,
Out and in,
With a turn of her head,
And a lift of her chin,
And a gleam of her eye,
And a twirl and a spin;
Sailing under
The breathless hush
Of the willows, and back
To the frozen rush;
Out to the island
And round the edge,
Skirting the rim
Of the crackling sedge,
Swerving close
To the poplar root,
And round the lake
On a single foot,
With a three, and an eight,
And a loop and a ring;

Where Mary glides,
The lake will sing!
Out in the mist
I hear her now
Under the frost
Of the willow-bough
Easily sailing,
Light and fleet,
With the song of the lake
Beneath her feet.

The Cataract of Lodore

Robert Southey

How does the water come down at
    Lodore?
    My little boy asked me thus, once
    on a time.
    Moreover, he task'd me to tell him
    in rhyme;
Anon at the word there first came one
    daughter,
    And then came another to second
    and third
The request of their brother, and hear
    how the water
Comes down at Lodore, with its rush
    and its roar,
As many a time they had seen it
    before.
So I told them in rhyme, for of rhymes
    I had store.
And 'twas in my vocation that thus I
    should sing,
Because I was laureate to them and
    the King.

From its sources which well
In the tarn on the fell,
From its fountain in the moun-
    tain,
Its rills and its gills,
Through moss and through
    brake,
It runs and it creeps,
For a while till it sleeps,
In its own little lake,
And thence at departing,
Awakening and starting,
It runs through the reeds,
And away it proceeds,
Through meadow and glade,
In sun and in shade,
And through the wood shelter,
Among crags in its flurry,
Helter-skelter — hurry-skurry.

How does the water come down at
    Lodore?
        Here it comes sparkling,
        And there it lies darkling;
        Here smoking and frothing,
        Its tumult and wrath in,
    It hastens along, conflicting, and
    strong,

Now striking and raging,
As if a war waging,
Its caverns and rocks among.
Rising and leaping,
Sinking and creeping,
Swelling and flinging,
Showering and springing,
Eddying and whisking,
Spouting and frisking,
Twining and twisting,
　　Around and around,
Collecting, disjecting,
　　With endless rebound;
Smiting and fighting,
A sight to delight in;
Confounding, astounding,
Dizzying and deafening the ear
with its sound.

Receding and speeding,
And shocking and rocking,
And darting and parting,
And threading and spreading,
And whizzing and hissing,
And dripping and skipping,
And whitening and brighten-
    ing,
And quivering and shivering,
And hitting and splitting,
And shining and twining,
And rattling and battling,
And shaking and quaking,
And pouring and roaring,
And waving and raving,
And tossing and crossing,
And flowing and growing,
And running and stunning,
And hurrying and skurrying,
And glittering and frittering,
And gathering and feathering,
And dinning and spinning,
And foaming and roaming,
And dropping and hopping,
And working and jerking,
And heaving and cleaving,
And thundering and flounder-
    ing;

And falling and crawling and sprawl-
    ing,
And driving and riving and striving,
And sprinkling and twinkling and
    wrinkling,
And sounding and bounding and
    rounding,
And bubbling and troubling and
    doubling,
Dividing and gliding and sliding,
And grumbling and rumbling and
    tumbling,
And clattering and battering and
    shattering;
And gleaming and steaming and
    streaming and beaming,
And rushing and flushing and brush-
    ing and gushing,
And flapping and rapping and clap-
    ping and slapping,
And curling and whirling and purling
    and twirling,
Retreating and beating and meeting
    and sheeting,
Delaying and straying and playing and
    spraying,
Advancing and prancing and glanc-
    ing and dancing,

Recoiling, turmoiling and toiling and
    boiling,
And thumping and flumping and
    bumping and jumping,
And dashing and flashing and splash-
    ing and clashing,—
And so never ending, but always
    descending,
Sounds and motions for ever and ever
    are blending,
All at once and all o'er, with a mighty
    uproar—
And this way the water comes down
    at Lodore.

The Brook

Alfred Tennyson

I come from haunts of coot and hern,
    I make a sudden sally,
And sparkle out among the fern,
    To bicker down a valley.

By thirty hills I hurry down,
    Or slip between the ridges,
By twenty thorps, a little town,
    And half a hundred bridges.

Till last by Philip's farm I flow
    To join the brimming river,
For men may come and men may go,
    But I go on forever.

I chatter over stony ways,
    In little sharps and trebles,
I bubble into eddying bays,
    I babble on the pebbles.

With many a curve my banks I fret
    By many a field and fallow,
And many a fairy foreland set
    With willow-weed and mallow.

I chatter, chatter, as I flow
    To join the brimming river,
For men may come and men may go,
    But I go on forever.

I wind about and in and out,
    With here a blossom sailing,
And here and there a lusty trout,
    And here and there a grayling,

And here and there a foamy flake
    Upon me, as I travel
With many a silvery water-break
    Above the golden gravel,

And draw them all along, and flow
    To join the brimming river,
For men may come and men may go,
    But I go on forever.

I steal by lawns and grassy plots,
　　I slide by hazel covers;
I move the sweet forget-me-nots
　　That grow for happy lovers.

I slip, I slide, I gloom, I glance,
　　Among my skimming swallows;
I make the netted sunbeam dance
　　Against my sandy shallows.

I murmur under moon and stars
　　In brambly wildernesses;
I linger by my shingly bars,
　　I loiter round my cresses;

And out again I curve and flow
　　To join the brimming river,
For men may come and men may go,
　　But I go on forever.

Duck's Ditty
Kenneth Grahame

All along the backwater,
   Through the rushes tall,
Ducks are a-dabbling,
   Up tails all!

Ducks' tails, drakes' tails,
   Yellow feet a-quiver,
Yellow bills all out of sight
   Busy in the river!

Slushy green undergrowth
   Where the roaches swim —
Here we keep our larder,
   Cool and full and dim.

Everyone for what he likes!
   We like to be
Heads down, tails up,
   Dabbling free!

High in the blue above
   Swifts whirl and call —
We are down a-dabbling,
   Up tails all!

Chanticleer
Katherine Tynan

Of all the birds from East to West
    That tuneful are and dear,
I love that farmyard bird the best,
    They call him Chanticleer.

Gold plume and copper plume,
    Comb of scarlet gay;
'Tis he that scatters night and gloom,
    And summons back the day!

He is the sun's brave herald
    Who, ringing his blithe horn,
Calls round a world dew-pearled
    The heavenly airs of morn.

Oh, clear gold, shrill and bold,
    He calls through creeping mist
The mountains from the night and cold
    To rose and amethyst.

He sets the birds to singing,
    And calls the flowers to rise;
The morning cometh, bringing
    Sweet sleep to heavy eyes.

Gold plume and silver plume,
　Comb of coral gay;
'Tis he packs off the night and gloom,
　And summons home the day.

Black fear he sends it flying,
　Black care he drives afar;
And creeping shadows sighing
　Before the morning star.

The birds of all the forest
　Have dear and pleasant cheer,
But yet I hold the rarest
　The farmyard Chanticleer.

Red cock and black cock,
　Gold cock or white,
The flower of all the feathered flock,
　He summons back the light!

The Chickadee
Ralph Waldo Emerson

Piped a tiny voice hard by,
Gay and polite, a cheerful cry,
"Chic-chicadee-dee!" Saucy note
Out of a sound heart and a merry throat,
As if it said, "Good day, good sir.
Fine afternoon, old passenger!
Happy to meet you in these places
When January brings new faces!"

The Woodpecker
Elizabeth Madox Roberts

The woodpecker pecked out a little round hole
And made him a house in the telephone pole.

One day when I watched he poked out his head,
And he had on a hood and a collar of red.

When the streams of rain pour out of the sky,
And the sparkles of lightning go flashing by,

And the big, big wheels of thunder roll,
He can snuggle back in the telephone pole.

The Runaway
Robert Frost

Once, when the snow of the year was beginning to fall,
We stopped by a mountain pasture to say "Whose colt?"
A little Morgan had one forefoot on the wall,
The other curled at his breast. He dipped his head
And snorted to us. And then he had to bolt.
We heard the miniature thunder where he fled
And we saw him or thought we saw him dim and gray,
Like a shadow against the curtain of falling flakes.
"I think the little fellow's afraid of the snow.
He isn't winter-broken. It isn't play
With the little fellow at all. He's running away.
I doubt if even his mother could tell him, 'Sakes,
It's only weather.' He'd think she didn't know.
Where is his mother? He can't be out alone."
And now he comes again with a clatter of stone
And mounts the wall again with whited eyes
And all his tail that isn't hair up straight.
He shudders his coat as if to throw off flies.
"Whoever it is that leaves him out so late,
When other creatures have gone to stall and bin,
Ought to be told to come and take him in."

The Sandpiper
Celia Thaxter

Across the narrow beach we flit,
   One little sandpiper and I,
And fast I gather, bit by bit,
   The scattered driftwood bleached and dry.
The wild waves reach their hands for it,
   The wild wind raves, the tide runs high,
As up and down the beach we flit, —
   One little sandpiper and I.

Above our heads the sullen clouds
   Scud black and swift across the sky;
Like silent ghosts in misty shrouds
   Stand out the white lighthouses high.
Almost as far as eye can reach
   I see the close-reefed vessels fly,
As fast we flit along the beach, —
   One little sandpiper and I.

I watch him as he skims along,
   Uttering his sweet and mournful cry.
He starts not at my fitful song,
   Nor flash of fluttering drapery.
He has no thought of any wrong;
   He scans me with a fearless eye:
Staunch friends are we, well tried and strong,
   The little sandpiper and I.

Comrade, where wilt thou be tonight,
    When the loosed storm breaks furiously?
My driftwood fire will burn so bright!
    To what warm shelter canst thou fly?
I do not fear for thee, though wroth
    The tempest rushes through the sky:
For are we not God's children both,
    Thou, little sandpiper, and I?

Connecticut Rondel
Marion Canby

He shakes his mane upon the breeze
And gallops through the grasses;
He does not like the encircling trees —
He likes to see what passes.

He trots along much at his ease
And snatches as he passes,
Then shakes his mane upon the breeze
And gallops through the grasses.

He does not like the buzz of bees
That fades and then repasses;
He loves the open swish of trees
And the wide hum of grasses;
He shakes his mane upon the breeze.

The Cowboy's Life
Attributed to James Barton Adams

The bawl of a steer,
To a cowboy's ear,
Is music of sweetest strain;
And the yelping notes
Of the gay coyotes
To him are a glad refrain.

For a kingly crown
In the noisy town
His saddle he wouldn't change;
No life so free
As the life we see
Way out on the Yaso range.

The rapid beat
Of his broncho's feet
On the sod as he speeds along,
Keeps living time
To the ringing rhyme
Of his rollicking cowboy song.

The winds may blow
And the thunder growl
Or the breezes may safely moan;—
A cowboy's life
Is a royal life,
His saddle his kingly throne.

The Faithless Flowers
Margaret Widdemer

I went this morning down to where the Johnny-jump-ups
    grow
Like naughty purple faces nodding in a row.
I stayed 'most all the morning there — I sat down on a
    stump
And watched and watched and watched them — and they
    never gave a jump!

And golden glow that stands up tall and yellow by the fence,
It doesn't glow a single bit — it's only just pretense —
I ran down after tea last night to watch them in the dark —
I had to light a match to see; they didn't give a spark!

And then the bouncing Bets don't bounce — I tried them
    yesterday,
I picked a big pink bunch down in the meadow where they
    stay,
I took a piece of string I had and tied them in a ball,
And threw them down as hard as hard — they never bounced
    at all!

And tiger lilies may look fierce, to meet them all alone,
All tall and black and yellowy and nodding by a stone,
But they're no more like tigers than the dogwood's like a dog,
Or bulrushes are like a bull or toadwort like a frog!

I like the flowers very much — they're pleasant as can be
For bunches on the table, and to pick and wear and see,
But still it doesn't seem quite fair — it does seem very
    queer —
They don't do what they're named for — not at any time
    of year!

The Mountain and The Squirrel

Ralph Waldo Emerson

The mountain and the squirrel
Had a quarrel,
And the former called the latter
    "Little prig;"
Bun replied,
"You are doubtless very big;
But all sorts of things and weather
Must be taken in together
To make up a year,
And a sphere.
And I think it no disgrace
To occupy my place.
If I'm not so large as you,
You are not so small as I,
And not half so spry:
I'll not deny you make
A very pretty squirrel track.
Talents differ; all is well and wisely put;
If I cannot carry forests on my back,
Neither can you crack a nut."

My Dog

Marchette Chute

His nose is short and scrubby;
   His ears hang rather low;
And he always brings the stick back,
   No matter how far you throw.

He gets spanked rather often
   For things he shouldn't do,
Like lying-on-beds, and barking,
   And eating up shoes when they're new.

He always wants to be going
   Where he isn't supposed to go.
He tracks up the house when it's snowing —
   Oh, puppy, I love you so.

A Kitten

Eleanor Farjeon

He's nothing much but fur
And two round eyes of blue,
He has a giant purr
And a midget mew.

He darts and pats the air,
He starts and cocks his ear,
When there is nothing there
For him to see and hear.

He runs around in rings,
But why we cannot tell;
With sideways leaps he springs
At things invisible —

Then half-way through a leap
His startled eyeballs close,
And he drops off to sleep
With one paw on his nose.

A Boy and a Pup
Arthur Guiterman

The boy wears a grin,
A scratch on his chin,
A wind-rumpled thatch,
A visible patch,
A cheek like a rose,
A frecklesome nose.

The pup, though he may
Be tawny as hay,
Is blithe as a song;
He gambols along
And waves to each friend
A wagglesome end.

With whistle and bark
They're off for a lark;
According to whim,
A hunt or a swim,
A tramp or a run
Or any old fun.

They don't care a jot
If school keeps or not,
When anything's up,
The boy and the pup —
That duo of joy,
A pup and a boy!

Puppy and I
A. A. Milne

I met a man as I went walking;
We got talking,
Man and I.
"Where are you going to, Man?" I said
  (I said to the Man as he went by).
"Down to the village, to get some bread.
  Will you come with me?" "No, not I."

I met a Horse as I went walking;
We got talking,
Horse and I.
"Where are you going to, Horse, to-day?"
  (I said to the Horse as he went by).
"Down to the village to get some hay.
  Will you come with me?" "No, not I."

I met a Woman as I went walking;
We got talking,
Woman and I.
"Where are you going to, Woman, so early?"
  (I said to the Woman as she went by).
"Down to the village to get some barley.
  Will you come with me?" "No, not I."

I met some Rabbits as I went walking;
We got talking,
Rabbits and I.
"Where are you going in your brown fur coats?"
   (I said to the Rabbits as they went by).
"Down to the village to get some oats.
   Will you come with us?" "No, not I."

I met a Puppy as I went walking;
We got talking,
Puppy and I.
"Where are you going this nice fine day?"
   (I said to the Puppy as he went by).
"Up in the hills to roll and play."
    "*I'll* come with you, Puppy," said I.

The Kitten Playing with the Falling Leaves
William Wordsworth

See the kitten on the wall
Sporting with the leaves that fall!
Withered leaves, one, two, and three,
From the lofty elder-tree.
Through the calm and frosty air
Of this morning bright and fair
Eddying round and round they sink
Softly, slowly. — One might think,
From the motions that are made,
Every little leaf conveyed
Some small fairy, hither tending,
To this lower world descending.
— But the kitten how she starts!
Crouches, stretches, paws, and darts:
First at one, and then its fellow,
Just as light, and just as yellow:
There are many now — now one —
Now they stop and there are none.
What intentness of desire
In her up-turned eye of fire!
With a tiger-leap half way,
Now she meets the coming prey.
Lets it go at last, and then
Has it in her power again.

Song of the Camels
William Shakespeare

Not born to the forest are we,
Not born to the plain,
To the grass and the shadowing tree
And the splashing of rain.
Only the sand we know
And the cloudless sky.
The mirage and the deep-sunk well
And the stars on high.

To the sound of our bells we came
With huge soft stride,
Kings riding upon our backs,
Slaves at our side.
Out of the east drawn on
By a dream and a star,
Seeking the hills and the groves
Where the fixed towns are.

Our goal was no palace gate,
No temple of old,
But a child on his mother's lap
In the cloudy cold.
The olives were windy and white,
Dust swirled through the town,
As all in their royal robes
Our masters knelt down.

To a Butterfly
William Wadsworth

I've watched you now a full half-hour,
Self-poised upon that yellow flower;
And, little butterfly! indeed
I know not if you sleep or feed.
How motionless! Not frozen seas
More motionless! And then
What joy awaits you, when the breeze
Has found you out among the trees,
And calls you forth again!

This plot of orchard-ground is ours;
My trees they are, my sister's flowers;
Here rest your wings when they are weary,
Here lodge as in a sanctuary!
Come often to us, fear no wrong;
Sit near us on the bough!
We'll talk of sunshine and of song,
And summer days, when we are young;
Sweet childish days, that were as long
As twenty days are now.

'Roads Go Ever Ever On'

J. R. R. Tolkien

Roads go ever ever on,
   Over rock and under tree,
By caves where sun has never shone,
   By streams that never find the sea;
Over snow by winter sown,
   And through the merry flowers of June,
Over grass and over stone,
   And under mountains in the moon.

Roads go ever ever on
   Under cloud and under star,
Yet feet that wandering have gone
   Turn at last to home afar.
Eyes that fire and sword have seen
   And horror in the halls of stone
Look at last on meadows green
   And trees and hills they long have known.

Sea Fever
John Masefield

I must go down to the seas again, to the lonely sea and the
    sky,
And all I ask is a tall ship and a star to steer her by,
And the wheel's kick and the wind's song and the white sail's
    shaking,
And a gray mist on the sea's face, and a gray dawn breaking.

I must go down to the seas again, for the call of the running
    tide
Is a wild call and a clear call that may not be denied;
And all I ask is a windy day with the white clouds flying,
And the flung spray and the blown spume, and the sea gulls
    crying.

I must go down to the seas again, to the vagrant gypsy life,
To the gull's way and the whale's way where the wind's like
    a whetted knife;
And all I ask is a merry yarn from a laughing fellow-rover,
And quiet sleep and a sweet dream when the long trick's over.

Roads

Rachel Field

A road might lead to anywhere —
   To harbor towns and quays,
Or to a witch's pointed house
   Hidden by bristly trees.
It might lead past the tailor's door,
   Where he sews with needle and thread,
Or by Miss Pim the milliner's,
   With her hats for every head.
It might be a road to a great, dark cave
   With treasure and gold piled high,
Or a road with a mountain tied to its end,
   Blue-humped against the sky.
Oh, a road might lead you anywhere —
   To Mexico or Maine.
But then, it might just fool you, and —
   Lead you back home again!

Goblin Feet
J. R. R. Tolkien

I am off down the road
Where the fairy lanterns glowed
And the little pretty flitter-mice are flying:
A slender band of gray
It runs creepily away
And the hedges and the grasses are a-sighing.
The air is full of wings,
And of blundery beetle-things
That warn you with their whirring and their humming.
O! I hear the tiny horns
Of enchanted leprechauns
And the padded feet of many gnomes a-coming!

O! the lights! O! the gleams! O! the little tinkly sounds!
O! the rustle of their noiseless little robes!
O! the echo of their feet — of their happy little feet!
O! their swinging lamps in little starlit globes.

I must follow in their train
Down the crooked fairy lane
Where the coney-rabbits long ago have gone,
And where silvery they sing
In a moving moonlit ring
All a-twinkle with the jewels they have on.
They are fading round the turn
Where the glow-worms palely burn
And the echo of their padding feet is dying!
O! it's knocking at my heart —
Let me go! O! let me start!
For the little magic hours are all a-flying.

O! the warmth! O! the hum! O! the colours in the dark!
O! the gauzy wings of golden honey-flies!
O! the music of their feet — of their dancing goblin feet!
O! the magic! O! the sorrow when it dies.

The Little Elf
John Kendrick Bangs

I met a little Elf man, once,
  Down where the lilies blow.
I asked him why he was so small,
  And why he didn't grow.

He slightly frowned, and with his eye
  He looked me through and through.
"I'm quite as big for me," said he,
  "As you are big for you."

The Elf and the Dormouse
Oliver Herford

Under a toadstool
  Crept a wee Elf,
Out of the rain
  To shelter himself.

Under the toadstool,
  Sound asleep,
Sat a big Dormouse
  All in a heap.

Trembled the wee Elf,
   Frightened, and yet
Fearing to fly away
   Lest he get wet.

To the next shelter —
   Maybe a mile!
Sudden the wee Elf
   Smiled a wee smile.

Tugged till the toadstool
   Toppled in two,
Holding it over him,
   Gaily he flew.

Soon he was safe home,
   Dry as could be.
Soon woke the Dormouse —
   "Good gracious me!

"Where is my toadstool?"
   Loud he lamented.
And that's how umbrellas
   First were invented.

The Plaint of the Camel

Charles Edward Carryl

Canary-birds feed on sugar and seed,
　Parrots have crackers to crunch;
And as for poodles, they tell me the noodles
　Have chickens and cream for their lunch.
　　But there's never a question
　　About MY digestion —
　　ANYTHING does for me!

Cats, you're aware, can repose in a chair,
Chickens can roost upon rails;
Puppies are able to sleep in a stable,
　And oysters can slumber in pails.
　　But no one supposes
　　A poor Camel dozes—
　　ANY PLACE does for me!

Lambs are enclosed where it's never exposed,
　Coops are constructed for hens;
Kittens are treated to houses well heated,
　And pigs are protected by pens.
　　But a Camel comes handy
　　Wherever it's sandy —
　　ANYWHERE does for me!

People would laugh if you rode a giraffe,
  Or mounted the back of an ox;
It's nobody's habit to ride on a rabbit,
  Or try to bestraddle a fox.
    But as for a Camel, he's
    Ridden by families —
    ANY LOAD does for me!

A snake is as round as a hole in the ground,
  And weasels are wavy and sleek;
And no alligator could ever be straighter
  Than lizards that live in a creek,
    But a Camel's all lumpy
    And bumpy and humpy —
    ANY SHAPE does for me!

Godfrey Gordon Gustavus Gore
William Brighty Rands

Godfrey Gordon Gustavus Gore —
No doubt you have heard the name before —
Was a boy who never would shut a door!

The wind might whistle, the wind might roar,
And teeth be aching and throats be sore,
But still he never would shut the door.

His father would beg, his mother implore,
"Godfrey Gordon Gustavus Gore,
We really *do* wish you would shut the door!"

Their hands they wring, their hair they tore;
But Godfrey Gordon Gustavus Gore
Was deaf as the buoy out at the Nore.

When he walked forth the folks would roar,
"Godfrey Gordon Gustavus Gore,
Why don't you think to shut the door?"

They rigged out a Shutter with sail and oar,
And threatened to pack off Gustavus Gore
On a voyage of penance to Singapore.

But he begged for mercy, and said, "No more!
Pray do not send me to Singapore
On a Shutter, and then I will shut the door!"

"You will?" said his parents; "then keep on shore!
But mind you do! For the plague is sore
Of a fellow that never will shut the door,
Godfrey Gordon Gustavus Gore!"

Eletelephony

Laura Elizabeth Richards

Once there was an elephant,
Who tried to use the telephant —
No! no! I mean an elephone
Who tried to use the telephone —
(Dear me! I am not certain quite
That even now I've got it right).

Howe'er it was, he got his trunk
Entangled in the telephunk;
The more he tried to get it free,
The louder buzzed the telephee —
(I fear I'd better drop the song
Of elephop and telephong!)

An Odd Fellow

Lewis Carroll

There was one who was famed for the number of things
    He forgot when he entered the ship:
His umbrella, his watch, all his jewels and rings,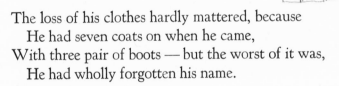
    And the clothes he had bought for the trip.

He had forty-two boxes, all carefully packed,
    With his name painted clearly on each;
But, since he omitted to mention the fact,
    They were all left behind on the beach.

The loss of his clothes hardly mattered, because
    He had seven coats on when he came,
With three pair of boots — but the worst of it was,
    He had wholly forgotten his name.

He would answer to "Hi!" or to any loud cry,
    Such as "Fry me!" or "Fritter my wig!"
To "What-you-may-call-um!" or "What-was-his-name!"
    But especially "Thing-um-a-jig!"

While, for those who preferred a more forcible word,
    He had different names from these:
His intimate friends called him "Candle-ends,"
    And his enemies "Toasted-cheese."

Pirate Don Durk of Dowdee
Mildred Meigs

Ho, for the Pirate Don Durk of Dowdee!
He was as wicked as wicked could be,
But oh, he was perfectly gorgeous to see!
   The Pirate Don Durk of Dowdee.

His conscience, of course, was black as a bat,
But he had a floppety plume on his hat
And when he went walking it jiggled — like that!
   The plume of the Pirate Dowdee.

His coat it was crimson and cut with a slash,
And often as ever he twirled his moustache,
Deep down in the ocean the mermaids went splash,
   Because of Don Durk of Dowdee.

Moreover, Dowdee had a purple tattoo,
And stuck in his belt where he buckled it through
Were a dagger, a dirk and a squizzamaroo
   For fierce was the Pirate Dowdee.

So fearful he was he would shoot at a puff,
And always at sea when the weather grew rough
He drank from a bottle and wrote on his cuff,
   Did Pirate Don Durk of Dowdee.

Oh, he had a cutlass that swung at his thigh
And he had a parrot called Pepperkin Pye,
And a zigzaggy scar at the end of his eye
   Had Pirate Don Durk of Dowdee.

He kept in a cavern, this buccaneer bold,
A curious chest that was covered with mould,
And all of his pockets were jingly with gold!
   Oh, jing! went the gold of Dowdee.

His conscience, of course, it was crook'd like a squash,
But both of his boots made a slickery slosh,
And he went through the world with a wonderful swash,
   Did Pirate Don Durk of Dowdee.

It's true he was wicked as wicked could be,
His sins they outnumbered a hundred and three,
But oh, he was perfectly gorgeous to see,
   The Pirate Don Durk of Dowdee.

The Owl and the Pussy-Cat

Edward Lear

I

The Owl and the Pussy-cat went to sea
    In a beautiful pea-green boat,
They took some honey, and plenty of money,
    Wrapped up in a five-pound note.
The Owl looked up to the stars above,
    And sang to a small guitar,
"O lovely Pussy! O Pussy, my love,
    What a beautiful Pussy you are,
        You are,
        You are!
    What a beautiful Pussy you are!"

II

Pussy said to the Owl, "You elegant fowl!
    How charmingly sweet you sing!
O let us be married! too long we have tarried:
    But what shall we do for a ring?"
They sailed away, for a year and a day,
    To the land where the Bong-tree grows
And there in a wood a Piggy-wig stood
    With a ring at the end of his nose,
        His nose,
        His nose,
    With a ring at the end of his nose.

III

"Dear Pig, are you willing to sell for one shilling
    Your ring?"Said the Piggy, "I will."
So they took it away, and were married next day
    By the Turkey who lives on the hill.
They dined on mince, and slices of quince,
    Which they ate with a runcible spoon;
And hand in hand, on the edge of the sand,
    They danced by the light of the moon,
        The moon,
        The moon,
They danced by the light of the moon.

The Tale of Custard the Dragon
Ogden Nash

Belinda lived in a little white house,
With a little black kitten and a little gray mouse,
And a little yellow dog and a little red wagon,
And a realio, trulio, little pet dragon.

Now the name of the little black kitten was Ink,
And the little gray mouse, she called her Blink,
And the little yellow dog was sharp as Mustard,
But the dragon was a coward, and she called him Custard.

Custard the dragon had big sharp teeth,
And spikes on top of him and scales underneath,
Mouth like a fireplace, chimney for a nose,
And realio, trulio daggers on his toes.

Belinda was as brave as a barrel full of bears,
And Ink and Blink chased lions down the stairs,
Mustard was as brave as a tiger in a rage,
But Custard cried for a nice safe cage.

Belinda tickled him, she tickled him unmerciful,
Ink, Blink and Mustard, they rudely called him Percival,
They all sat laughing in the little red wagon
At the realio, trulio, cowardly dragon.

Belinda giggled till she shook the house,
And Blink said Weeek! which is giggling for a mouse,
Ink and Mustard rudely asked his age,
When Custard cried for a nice safe cage.

Suddenly, suddenly they heard a nasty sound,
And Mustard growled, and they all looked around.
Meowch! cried Ink, and Ooh! cried Belinda,
For there was a pirate, climbing in the winda.

Pistol in his left hand, pistol in his right,
And he held in his teeth a cutlass bright,
His beard was black, one leg was wood;
It was clear that the pirate meant no good.

Belinda paled, and she cried Help! Help!
But Mustard fled with a terrified yelp,
Ink trickled down to the bottom of the household,
And little mouse Blink strategically mouseholed.

But up jumped Custard, snorting like an engine,
Clashed his tail like irons in a dungeon,
With a clatter and a clank and a jangling squirm
He went at the pirate like a robin at a worm.

The pirate gaped at Belinda's dragon,
And gulped some grog from his pocket flagon,
He fired two bullets, but they didn't hit,
And Custard gobbled him, every bit.

Belinda embraced him, Mustard licked him,
No one mourned for his pirate victim.
Ink and Blink in glee did gyrate
Around the dragon that ate the pyrate.

Belinda still lives in her little white house,
With her little black kitten and her little gray mouse,
And her little yellow dog and her little red wagon,
And her realio, trulio, little pet dragon.

Belinda is as brave as a barrel full of bears,
And Ink and Blink chase lions down the stairs.
Mustard is as brave as a tiger in a rage,
But Custard keeps crying for a nice safe cage.

Jonathan Bing
Beatrice Curtis Brown

Poor old Jonathan Bing
Went out in his carriage to visit the King,
But everyone pointed and said, "Look at that!
Jonathan Bing has forgotten his hat!"
(He'd forgotten his hat!)

Poor old Jonathan Bing,
Went home and put on a new hat for the King,
But up by the palace a soldier said, "Hi!
You can't see the King; you've forgotten your tie!"
(He'd forgotten his tie!)

Poor old Jonathan Bing
He put on a *beautiful* tie for the King,
But when he arrived an Archbishop said, "Ho!
You can't come to court in pyjamas, you know!"

Poor old Jonathan Bing
Went home and addressed a short note to the King:
    If you please will excuse me
    I won't come to tea;
    For home's the best place for
    All people like me!

A Tragic Story

Albert Von Chamisso
Translated by William Makepeace Thackeray

There lived a sage in days of yore,
And he a handsome pigtail wore;
But wondered much, and sorrowed more,
Because it hung behind him.

He mused upon this curious case,
And swore he'd change the pigtail's place,
And have it hanging at his face,
Not dangling there behind him.

Says he, "The mystery I've found, —
I'll turn me round," — he turned him round,
But still it hung behind him.

Then round and round, and out and in,
All day the puzzled sage did spin;
In vain — in mattered not a pin —
The pigtail hung behind him.

And right and left, and roundabout,
And up and down and in and out
He turned; but still the pigtail stout
Hung steadily behind him.

And though his efforts never slack,
And though he twist, and twirl, and tack,
Alas! still faithful to his back,
The pigtail hangs behind him.

The Peppery Man

Arthur Macy

The Peppery Man was cross and thin;
He scolded out and scolded in;
He shook his fist, his hair he tore;
He stamped his feet and slammed the door.

   Heigh ho, the Peppery Man,
   The rabid, crabbed Peppery Man!
   Oh, never since the world began
   Was anyone like the Peppery Man.

His ugly temper was so sour
He often scolded for an hour;
He gnashed his teeth and stormed and scowled,
He snapped and snarled and yelled and howled.

He wore a fierce and savage frown;
He scolded up and scolded down;
He scolded over field and glen,
And then he scolded back again.

His neighbors, when they heard his roars,
Closed their blinds and locked their doors,
Shut their windows, sought their beds,
Stopped their ears and covered their heads.

He fretted, chafed, and boiled and fumed;
With fiery rage he was consumed,
And no one knew, when he was vexed,
What in the world would happen next.

Heigh ho, the Peppery Man,
The rabid, crabbed Peppery Man!
Oh, never since the world began
Was anyone like the Peppery Man.

A Nautical Ballad

Charles Edward Carryl

A capital ship for an ocean trip,
   Was the Walloping Window blind.
No gale that blew dismayed her crew,
   Nor troubled the captain's mind.

The man at the wheel was taught to feel
   Contempt for the wildest blow;
And it often appeared—when the weather had cleared—
   He had been in his bunk below.

The boatswain's mate was very sedate,
   Yet fond of amusement, too;
And he played hopscotch with the starboard watch,
   While the captain tickled the crew.

And the gunner we had was apparently mad,
   For he sat on the after rail
And fired salutes with the captain's boots
   In the teeth of the booming gale.

The captain sat on the commodore's hat,
    And dined in a royal way,
Off toasted pigs and pickles and figs
    And gunnery bread each day.

The cook was Dutch and behaved as such,
    For the diet he gave the crew
Was a number of tons of hot cross-buns,
    Served up with sugar and glue.

All nautical pride we laid aside,
    And we cast our vessel ashore,
On the Gulliby Isles, where the Poo-Poo smiles
    And the Rumpletum-Bunders roar.

We sat on the edge of a sandy ledge,
    And shot at the whistling bee:
And the cinnamon bats wore waterproof hats,
    As they danced by the sounding sea.

On Rug-gub bark, from dawn till dark,
    We fed, till we all had grown
Uncommonly shrunk; when a Chinese junk
    Came in from the Torrible Zone.

She was stubby and square, but we didn't much care,
    So we cheerily put to sea;
And we left the crew of the junk to chew
    The bark of the Rug-gub tree.

New England's Chevy Chase
(April 19, 1775)

Edward Everett Hale

'Twas the dead of the night. By the pineknot's red light
    Brooks lay, half-asleep, when he heard the alarm,—
Only this, and no more, from a voice at the door:
    "The Red-Coats are out, and have passed Phip's farm."

Brooks was booted and spurred; he said never a word:
    Took his horn from its peg, and his gun from the rack;
To the cold midnight air he led out his white mare,
    Strapped the girths and the bridle, and sprang to her
      back.

Up the North Country road at her full pace she strode,
    Till Brooks reined her up at John Tarbell's to say,
"We have got the alarm,—they have left Phip's farm;
    You rouse the East Precinct, and I'll go this way."

John called his hired man, and they harnessed the span;
  They roused Abram Garfield, and Abram called me:
"Turn out right away; let no minute-man stay;
  The Red-Coats have landed at Phip's," says he.

By the Powder-House Green seven others fell in;
  At Nahum's the men from the Saw-Mill came down;
So that when Jabez Bland gave the word of command,
  And said, "Forward, march!" there marched forward
  THE TOWN.

Parson Wilderspin stood by the side of the road,
  And he took off his hat, and he said, "Let us pray!
O Lord, God of might, let thine angels of light
  Lead thy children to-night to the glories of day!
And let thy stars fight all the foes of the Right
  As the stars fought of old against Sisera."

And from heaven's high arch those stars blessed our march,
  Till the last of them faded in twilight away;
And with morning's bright beam, by the banks of the stream
  Half the country marched in, and we heard Davis say:

"On the King's own highway I may travel all day,
  And no man hath warrant to stop me," says he;
"I've no man that's afraid, and I'll march at their head."
  Then he turned to the boys, "Forward, march! Follow
  me."

And we marched as he said, and the Fifer he played
  The old "White Cockade," and he played it right well.
We saw Davis fall dead, but no man was afraid;
  That bridge we'd have had, though a thousand men fell.

This opened the play, and it lasted all day.
  We made Concord too hot for the Red-Coats to stay;
Down the Lexington way we stormed, black, white, and
    gray
  We were first in the feast, and were last in the fray.

They would turn in dismay, as red wolves turn at bay.
  They levelled, they fired, they charged up the road.
Cephas Willard fell dead; he was shot in the head
  As he knelt by Aunt Prudence's well-sweep to load.

John Danforth was hit just in Lexington Street,
  John Bridge at that lane where you cross Beaver Falls,
And Winch and the Snows just above John Munroe's—
  Swept away by one swoop of the big cannon-balls.

I took Bridge on my knee, but he said, "Don't mind me;
Fill your horn from mine,—let me lie where I be.
Our fathers," says he, "that their sons might be free,
Left their king on his throne, and came over the sea;
And that man is a knave, or a fool who, to save
His life for a minute, would live like a slave."

Well, all would not do! There were men good as new,—
   From Rumford, from Saugus, from towns far away,—
Who filled up quick and well for each soldier that fell;
   And we drove them, and drove them, and drove them,
      all day.
We knew, every one, it was war that begun,
When that morning's marching was only half done.

In the hazy twilight, at the coming of night,
   I crowded three buckshot and one bullet down.
'Twas my last charge of lead; and I aimed her and said,
   "Good luck to you, lobsters, in old Boston Town."

In a barn at Milk Row, Ephraim Bates and Munroe,
   And Baker, and Abram, and I made a bed.
We had mighty sore feet, and we'd nothing to eat;
   But we'd driven the Red-Coats, and Amos, he said:
"It's the first time," says he, "that it's happened to me
   To march to the sea by this road where we've come;
But confound this whole day, but we'd all of us say
   We'd rather have spent it this way than to home."

The hunt had begun with the dawn of the sun,
   And night saw the wolf driven back to his den.
And never since then, in the memory of men,
   Has the Old Bay State seen such a hunting again.

Paul Revere's Ride
(April 18-19, 1775)

Henry Wadsworth Longfellow

Listen my children, and you shall hear
Of the midnight ride of Paul Revere,
On the eighteenth of April, in seventy-five;
Hardly a man is now alive
Who remembers that famous day and year.

He said to his friend, "If the British march
By land or sea from the town to-night,
Hang a lantern aloft in the belfry arch
Of the North Church tower as a signal light,—
One, if by land, and two, if by sea;
And I on the opposite shore will be,
Ready to ride and spread the alarm
Through every Middlesex village and farm,
For the country folk to be up and to arm."

Then he said, "Good night!" and with muffled oar
Silently rowed to the Charlestown shore,
Just as the moon rose over the bay,
Where swinging wide at her moorings lay
The Somerset, British man-of-war;
A phantom ship, with each mast and spar
Across the moon like a prison bar,
And a huge black hulk, that was magnified
By its own reflection in the tide.

Meanwhile, his friend, through alley and street,
Wanders and watches with eager ears,
Till in the silence around him he hears
The muster of men at the barrack door,
The sound of arms, and the tramp of feet,
And the measured tread of the grenadiers,
Marching down to their boats on the shore.

Then he climbed the tower of the old North Church,
By the wooden stairs, with stealthy tread,
To the belfry-chamber overhead,
And startled the pigeons from their perch
On the sombre rafters, that round him made
Masses and moving shapes of shade,—
By the trembling ladder, steep and tall,
To the highest window in the wall,
Where he paused to listen and look down
A moment on the roofs of the town,
And the moonlight flowing over all.

Beneath, in the churchyard, lay the dead,
In their night-encampment on the hill,
Wrapped in silence so deep and still
That he could hear, like a sentinel's tread,
The watchful night-wind, as it went
Creeping along from tent to tent,
And seeming to whisper, "All is well!"
A moment only he feels the spell
Of the place and the hour, and the secret dread

Of the lonely belfry and the dead;
For suddenly all his thoughts are bent
On a shadowy something far away,
Where the river widens to meet the bay,—
A line of black that bends and floats
On the rising tide, like a bridge of boats.

Meanwhile, impatient to mount and ride,
Booted and spurred, with a heavy stride
On the opposite shore walked Paul Revere.
Now he patted his horse's side,
Now gazed at the landscape far and near
Then, impetuous, stamped the earth,
And turned and tightened his saddle-girth;
But mostly he watched with eager search
The belfry-tower of the Old North Church,
As it rose above the graves on the hill,
Lonely and spectral and sombre and still.
And lo! as he looks, on the belfry's height
A glimmer, and then a gleam of light!
He springs to the saddle, the bridle he turns,
But lingers and gazes, till full on his sight
A second lamp in the belfry burns!

A hurry of hoofs in a village street,
A shape in the monlight, a bulk in the dark,
And beneath, from the pebbles, in passing, a spark
Struck out by a steed flying fearless and fleet:

That was all! And yet, through the gloom and the light,
The fate of a nation was riding that night;
And the spark struck out by that steed, in his flight,
Kindled the land into flame with its heat.

He has left the village and mounted the steep,
And beneath him, tranquil and broad and deep,
Is the Mystic, meeting the ocean tides;
And under the alders that skirt its edge,
Now soft on the sand, now loud on the ledge,
Is heard the tramp of his steed as he rides.

It was twelve by the village clock,
When he crossed the bridge into Medford town.
He heard the crowing of the cock,
And the barking of the farmer's dog,
And felt the damp of the river fog,
That rises after the sun goes down.

It was one by the village clock,
When he galloped into Lexington.
He saw the gilded weathercock
Swing in the moonlight as he passed.
And the meeting-house windows, blank and bare,
Gaze at him with a spectral glare,
As if they already stood aghast
At the bloody work they would look upon.

It was two by the village clock,
When he came to the bridge in Concord town.
He heard the bleating of the flock,
And the twitter of birds among the trees,
And felt the breath of the morning breeze
Blowing over the meadows brown.
And one was safe and asleep in his bed
Who at the bridge would be first to fall,
Who that day would be lying dead,
Pierced by a British musket-ball.

You know the rest. In the books you have read,
How the British Regulars fired and fled,—
How the farmers gave them ball for ball,
From behind each fence and farmyard wall,
Chasing the red-coats down the lane,
Then crossing the fields to emerge again
Under the trees at the turn of the road,
And only pausing to fire and load.

So through the night rode Paul Revere;
And so through the night went his cry of alarm
To every Middlesex village and farm,—
A cry of defiance and not of fear,
A voice in the darkness, a knock at the door,
And a word that shall echo forevermore!

For, borne on the night-wind of the Past,
Through all our history, to the last,
In the hour of darkness and peril and need,
The people will waken and listen to hear
The hurrying hoof-beats of that steed,
And the midnight message of Paul Revere.

If—
Rudyard Kipling

If you can keep your head when all about you
    Are losing theirs and blaming it on you;
If you can trust yourself when all men doubt you,
    But make allowance for their doubting too;
If you can wait and not be tired by waiting,
    Or, being lied about, don't deal in lies,
Or, being hated, don't give way to hating,
    And yet don't look too good, nor talk too wise;

If you can dream — and not make dreams your master;
    If you can think — and not make thoughts your aim;
If you can meet with triumph and disaster
    And treat those two imposters just the same;
If you can bear to hear the truth you've spoken
    Twisted by knaves to make a trap for fools,
Or watch the things you gave your life to broken,
    And stoop and build 'em up with wornout tools;

If you can make one heap of all your winnings
    And risk it on one turn of pitch-and-toss,
And lose, and start again at your beginnings
    And never breathe a word about your loss;
If you can force your heart and nerve and sinew
    To serve your turn long after they are gone,
And so hold on when there is nothing in you
    Except the Will which says to them: "Hold on";

If you can talk with crowds and keep your virtue,
    Or walk with kings — nor lose the common touch;
If neither foes nor loving friends can hurt you;
    If all men count with you, but none too much;
If you can fill the unforgiving minute
    With sixty seconds' worth of distance run —
Yours is the Earth and everything that's in it,
    And — which is more — you'll be a Man, my son!

Acknowledgments

The editor and the publisher have made every effort to trace the owner-ship of all copyrighted material and to secure permission from holders of such poems. In the event of any question arising as to the use of any material the publisher and editor, while expressing regret for inadver-tent error, will be pleased to make the necessary corrections in future printings. Thanks are due to the following authors, publishers, publica-tions and agents for permission to use the material indicated.

APPLETON-CENTURY-CROFTS, Educational Division, Meredith Corporation for "The Little Elf" by John Kendrick Bangs from *St. Nicholas,* 1893.

BASIL BLACKWELL & MOTT LTD. for "Goblin Feet" by J. R. R. Tolkien.

THE CHRISTIAN SCIENCE MONITOR for "Jack Frost" by Helen Bayley Davis.

DODD, MEAD & COMPANY, INC. for "I Meant to Do My Work Today" from *The Lonely Dancer* by Richard Le Gallienne; "A Vagabond Song" from *Bliss Carman's Poems.*

DOUBLEDAY AND COMPANY, INC., for "If" from *Rewards and Fairies* by Rudyard Kipling, copyright 1910 by Rudyard Kipling and with permission by Mrs. George Bambridge, Macmillan Co., Ltd., and the Macmillan Company of Canada Ltd.

E. P. DUTTON & CO., INC., for "Halfway Down" and "Puppy and I" by A. A. Milne from *When We were Very Young* and with permission by Methuen & Co., Ltd. Copyright 1924 by E. P. Dutton & Co., Inc., renewal 1952 by A. A. Milne. "My Dog" from *Around and About* by Marchette Chute, copyright 1932 © 1960 by Marchette Chute.

MRS. ARTHUR GUITERMAN for "A Boy and a Pup" from *The Laughing Muse* and "House Blessing" from *Death and General Putnam* by Arthur Guiterman.

HARCOURT, BRACE & WORLD, INC., for "The Faithless Flowers" from *Little Girl and Boy Land* by Margaret Widdemer, copyright 1924 by Harcourt, Brace and World, Inc.; renewed 1952 by Margaret Widdemer Schauffler.

HARPER & ROW, PUBLISHERS, INC. for "Old Log House" from *A World to Know* by James S. Tippett. Copyright 1933 Harper & Brothers; renewed 1961 by Martha K. Tippett.

HOLT, RINEHART AND WINSTON, INC. for "The Runaway" from *Complete Poems of Robert Frost.* Copyright 1923 by Holt, Rinehart and Winston, Inc. Copyright 1951 by Robert Frost. "Two in a Bed" from *Five Going On Six* by A. B. Ross. Copyright 1927 by Holt, Rinehart and Winston, Inc.

HOUGHTON MIFFLIN COMPANY for "Roads Go Ever Ever On" from *The Hobbit* by J. R. R. Tolkien. Also for "I Want to Know" and "The Sun" by John Drinkwater; "The Mountain and the Squirrel" and "The Chickadee" by Ralph Waldo Emerson; "The Plaint of the Camel" and "A Nautical Ballad," by Charles Edward Carryl; "The Sandpiper" by Celia Thaxter; "Paul Revere's Ride" by Henry Wadsworth Longfellow.

BARBARA BOYDEN JORDAN for "Mud" by Polly Chase Boyden, from *Child Life Magazine,* copyright 1930, 1958 by Rand McNally & Company.

J. B. LIPPINCOTT COMPANY for "Song for a Little House" from *Songs for a Little House* by Christopher Morley. Copyright 1917, 1945 by Christopher Morley; "School-bell" by Eleanor Farjeon, copyright 1938 by Eleanor Farjeon; copyright renewed 1966 by Gervase Farjeon; "A Kitten" by Eleanor Farjeon, copyright 1933, 1961 by Eleanor Farjeon (both from *Poems for Children* by Eleanor Farjeon).

LITTLE, BROWN AND COMPANY for "The Tale of Custard the Dragon" from *Verses From 1929 On* by Ogden Nash, copyright 1936 by Ogden Nash, and with permission by J. M. Dent & Sons Ltd.; "Eletelephony" from *Tirra Lirra* by Laura E. Richards, copyright 1935 by Laura E. Richards.

LOTHROP, LEE & SHEPARD CO., INC. and Curtis-Brown Ltd., for "Jonathan Bing Visits the King" from *Jonathan Bing* by Beatrice Curtis Brown. Copyright 1936 by Oxford University Press. Copyright © 1964 by Beatrice Curtis Brown.

THE MACMILLAN COMPANY for "White Fields" from *Collected Poems* by James Stephens; "Skating" from *Pillicock Hill* by Herbert Asquith; "Sea Fever" from *Collected Poems* by John Masefield; "Roads" from *The Pointed People* by Rachel Field.

G. P. PUTNAM'S SONS for "Hiding" from *Everything and Anything* by Dorothy Aldis. Copyright 1925, 1926, 1927 by Dorothy Aldis.

CHARLES SCRIBNER'S SONS for "Ducks Ditty" from *The Wind in the Willows* by Kenneth Grahame. "The Land of Story Books", "The Land of Counterpane" and "My Shadow" from *A Child's Garden of Verses* by Robert Louis Stevenson.

SHEED & WARD, INC., for "Daddy Fell Into the Pond" from *Daddy Fell Into the Pond and other Poems* by Alfred Noyes, copyright 1952, Sheed & Ward, Inc.

THE SOCIETY OF AUTHORS and Miss Pamela Hinkson for "Chanticleer" by Katherine Tynan.

THE VIKING PRESS, INC. for "The Woodpecker" from *Under the Tree* by Elizabeth Madox Roberts, copyright 1922 by B. W. Huebsch, Inc., renewed 1950 by Ivor S. Roberts.

YALE UNIVERSITY PRESS for "A Comparison" from *Songs for Parents* by John Farrar, copyright © 1921 by Yale University Press.